Light

Written by Paul Bennett

Wayland

Boxes   Journeys
Changes   Light
Colours   Patterns
Holes   Wheels

Picture acknowledgements

The publishers would like to thank the following for allowing their photographs to be reproduced in this book: Bruce Coleman Ltd 5 (Konrad Wothe), 7 (Johnny Johnson), 12 (below/Peter A. Hinchcliffe), 17 (below/Hector Rivarola); Eye Ubiquitous 23 (above/Peter Blake); Chris Fairclough Colour Library 16; Sally and Richard Greenhill 20 (below); The Hutchison Library 26 (middle); Science Photo Library 12 (above), 21, 28 (below); Tony Stone Worldwide 4 (below); 6, 8, 10 (below), 11, 14, 19 (above), 20 (above), 22, 26 (top), 29; Topham 25 (below); the Wayland Picture Library 9, 19 (below), 23 (below): Tim Woodcock 4 (above), 10 (above), 18, 27, 28 (above/Keith Ackford); ZEFA 13, 15, 17 (above), 24, 25 (above), 26 (below).

Cover photography by Zul Mukhida, organized by Zoë Hargreaves. With thanks to Stanford Infants School.

First published in 1992 by
Wayland (Publishers) Ltd
61 Western Road, Hove
East Sussex BN3 1JD, England

© Copyright 1992 Wayland (Publishers) Ltd

Editor: Francesca Motisi
Designers: Jean and Robert Wheeler
Picture research: Paul Bennett

Consultant: Sue Yearley is currently a senior lecturer in Education Studies at Brighton Polytechnic. Her previous teaching experience includes primary, secondary and learning support. She has particular interest in children with special educational needs. Sue wrote the notes for parents and teachers and provided the topic web.

British Library Cataloguing in Publication Data
Bennett Paul.
Light. – (Criss Cross Series)
I. Title II. Series
535

ISBN 0-7502-0401-X

Typeset by DJS Fotoset Ltd, Brighton, Sussex
Printed and bound in Italy by L.E.G.O. S.p.A., Vicenza

Contents

Words that appear in **bold** in the text are explained in the glossary on page 32.

Light from the sun

During the day, our light comes from the sun. The sun is brightest in the middle of the day. When it is sunny, there are shadows.

As the sun goes down, the light fades and day turns into night. At **dawn**, the sun comes up and it is no longer dark.

At night, the moon gives us some light. The light from this **full moon** shines brightly on the water.

Light in the sky

Have you seen lightning during a thunderstorm?
Lightning is an electric flash from the clouds and
can be very **spectacular**.

6

What are these lights in the night sky?
They are called **auroras** and they move as well as
glow. They can be seen in the far north and far
south of the world.

When it is too bright

Do you wear sun-glasses when the sun is bright?
The sun is at its strongest and hottest in the middle
of the day.

In the summer, many people wear hats to help keep the sun out of their eyes and to protect their heads. Looking directly at the sun will damage your eyes.

Turn on the light

What do you do when there is not enough light? This boy is reading a book with an electric light on. Look around your home and count the number of lights you have.

At night, the streets are lit by street lamps, and drivers turn on their **headlights**. In many towns and cities, **advertisements** also light up the streets.

A ship in **dry dock** is lit up by electric lights so that people can work on it all night.

Animal lights

Some animals can make their own light. Fireflies and glow-worms are types of beetles that can make the ends of their bodies light up. They come out at night and use the lights to signal to each other.

This jellyfish lives deep in the sea where it is very dark. Some fish, that live at the bottom of the sea, are also able to make light.

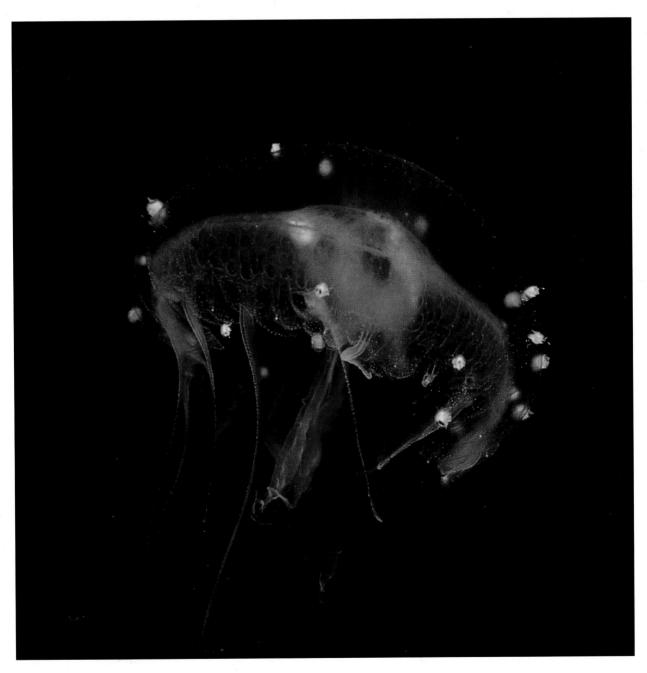

Rainbows

When the sunlight shines through the rain, a rainbow appears like magic. Do you know which colours make a rainbow? If you look carefully, you will see red, orange, yellow, green, blue, indigo and violet. These colours are called a **spectrum**.

A specially-shaped piece of glass called a
prism will make a spectrum from an electric
light. Raindrops and prisms show that
what seems to be white light is really made
up of lots of colours.

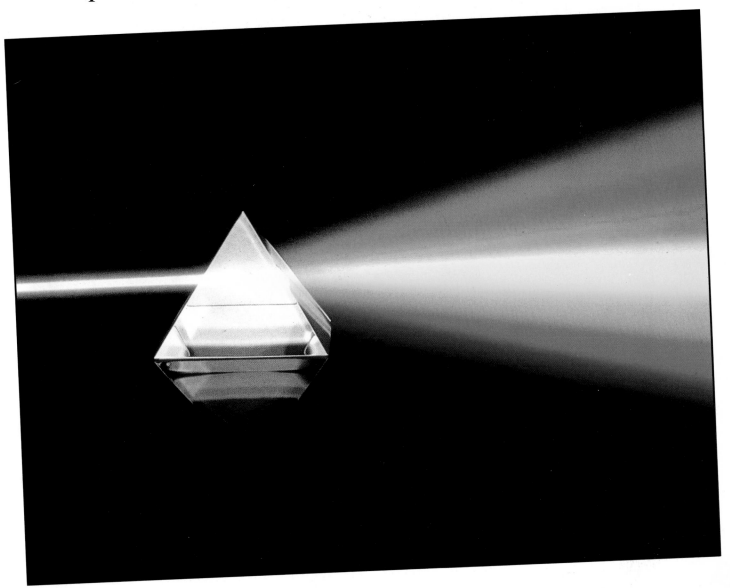

Magnifying light

Have you ever wanted to look closely at something small?

A magnifying glass helps to make things look bigger.

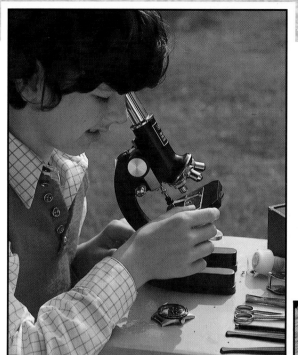

A microscope is a special sort of magnifying glass used for looking at tiny things. This is what a moth's wing looks like under a microscope.

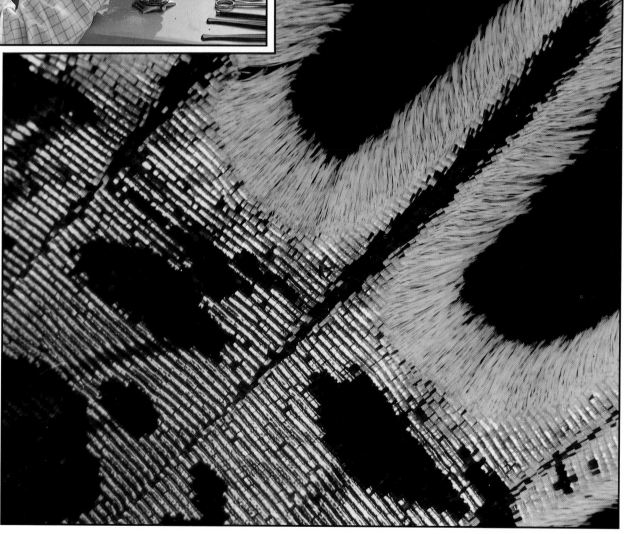

Reflecting light

Mirrors and shiny metal **reflect** light very well. You can see your face in a spoon. This boy is able to see his painted face in a mirror. It is called a reflection. When do you look in a mirror?

Some sun-glasses are like mirrors. Windows and water can reflect light too. Sometimes it is hard to see what is real, and what is a reflection, because the reflection is so clear.

Distorting light

Ripples in water can **distort** a reflection so that it is no longer clear.

Have you ever looked at yourself in a distorting mirror at a fairground? These mirrors can stretch or squash your reflection into funny shapes.

Light can bend when it passes through water. This is a straight straw that looks bent. Look to see if this happens next time you have a drink with a straw.

Shine a light

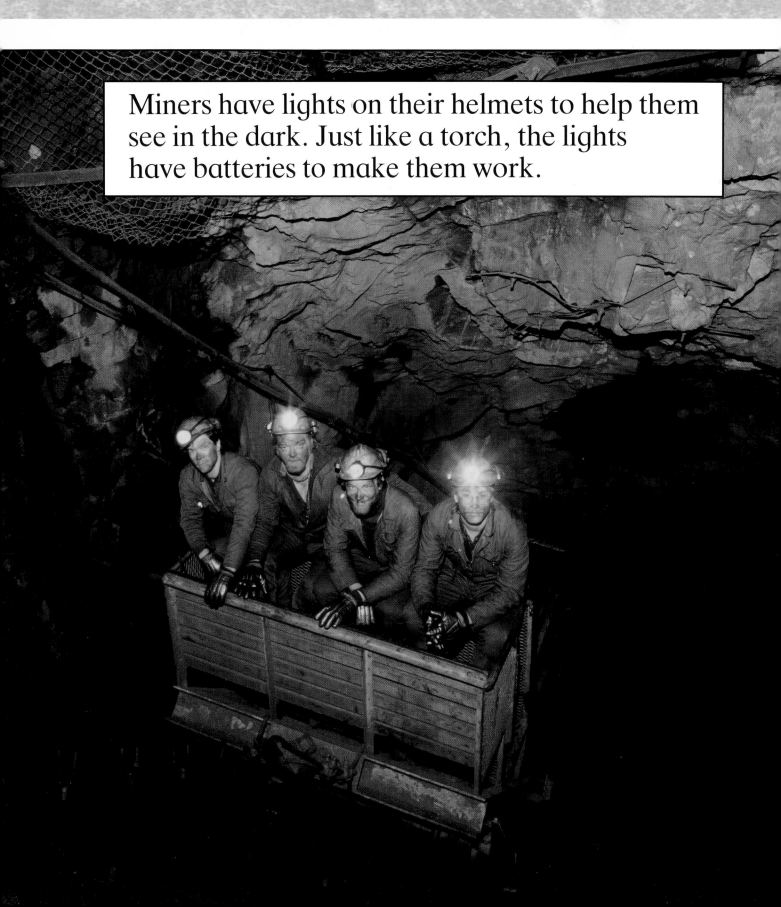

Miners have lights on their helmets to help them see in the dark. Just like a torch, the lights have batteries to make them work.

The light shining on these skaters is called a spotlight. They are also used in theatres.

This woman is using a **lightbox** to shine a light through some **slides**. She is looking through a magnifying glass to make the pictures look bigger.

Warning lights

Lights are used to warn people of danger. A lighthouse flashes a light to warn ships not to come too near the rocks.

The place where several roads meet often has traffic lights. Cars, trucks and buses that travel along the road must stop when the light shows red.

These fire engines have flashing lights to warn the other traffic that they need to get to a fire quickly. Think of some other cars that use flashing warning lights.

Festival lights

◀ Lights help to make festivals special. At Christmas, Christians put lights on Christmas trees.

Hindus have a festival of lights called Diwali. ▶

◀ People who follow the Jewish religion light candles at their festival called Hanukkah.

You can tell how old a person is by counting the number of candles on their birthday cake. How many candles will you have to blow out on your next birthday cake?

Light show

◀ These children are waving **sparklers** at a fireworks party.

Fireworks like these light up the sky on special occasions. They make coloured flames, sparks and smoke. ▶

A **laser** produces a very thin beam of light. Laser light is used for special effects in films, at discos and at pop concerts.

Notes for parents and teachers

The main concepts in this book are natural and artificial light, and the great variety of ways in which light is used for work and play.

This is a topic which can raise awareness of cause and effect, and the many ways in which our everyday lives are dependent upon light in all its forms.

Language
● Children will be able to talk about their experiences of celebrations and festivals.
● We have many light-related phrases in our language which can be discussed and extended e.g. *light at the end of the tunnel, to cast light upon the subject* etc.
● Children also need to recognize that we use the same word as a contrast with heavy (i.e. as a noun and an adjective).
● There are many references in literature to this topic, some poems for example: *Night* by William Blake, *The Moon* by Robert Louis Stevenson, *Months of the Year* by Sara Coleridge and *Good Morning* by Eleanor Farjeon.

Maths
● Young children will have little idea of the measurement of time.
●They can be helped towards an understanding of measuring hours, days, weeks etc. through keeping records of daily recurring activities in their own lives e.g. "I wake up at . . ." etc.
● A 24 hour timeline can be linked to this, showing hours of daylight and darkness.
● Awareness of our planet's movement in relation to the sun can be introduced by keeping measurements of lengths of shadows taken at different times of day.

Science
● The effect of light on animals and plants can be explored. All living things need sunlight to grow.
● Children can learn through playing with prisms, magnifying glasses and mirrors some of the physics of light, and can also learn about powering artificial light through setting up a simple circuit with light bulb.

History
● Through examining artefacts such as candlesticks and lanterns children can begin to think about life without electric light.

Geography
● Through their own experience of seasonal weather changes, and climate changes when holidaying or living in different climates, children can begin to understand the effects of heat from the sun.

P.E. Dance/Drama
● Some fun effects of light, such as distortions and reflections could be used as the starting point for body shapes.

Art
● Lots of scope here for work using light/dark shades of colour and to begin to appreciate their aesthetic effects.
● Make shadow puppets.

Technology
● Make sundials and candle-clocks.
● Make a lighthouse or emergency vehicle with a flashing light.

Music
● Plenty to choose from here, from familiars such as *Twinkle Twinkle Little Star* to the *Moonlight Sonata* by Beethoven and *Morning* from Grieg's Peer Gynt.

R.E.
● Most religions use light as a metaphor and for festivals. Children can be introduced to different beliefs through the common experience of lighting candles for celebration.

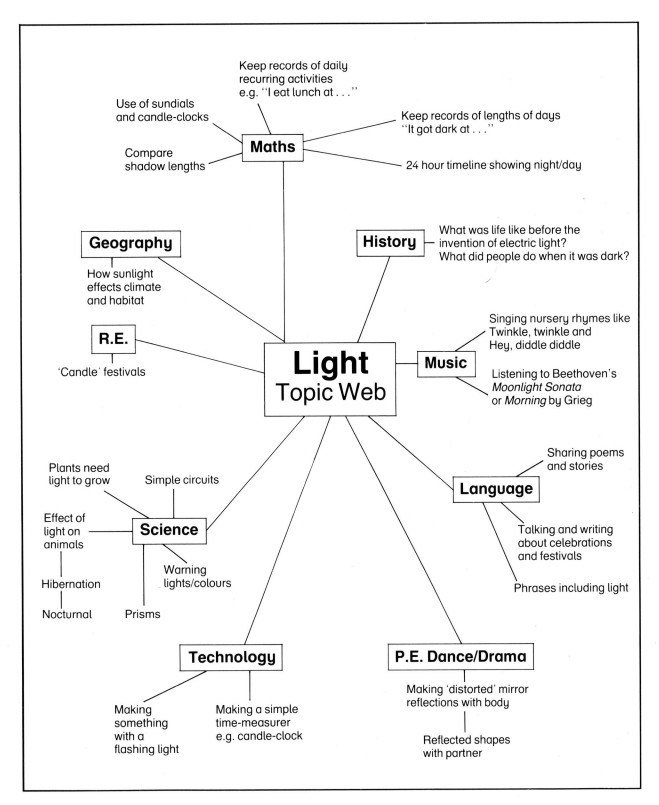

Keep records of daily
recurring activities
e.g. "I eat lunch at . . ."

Use of sundials
and candle-clocks

Maths

Keep records of lengths of days
"It got dark at . . ."

Compare
shadow lengths

24 hour timeline showing night/day

Geography

History

What was life like before the
invention of electric light?
What did people do when it was dark?

How sunlight
effects climate
and habitat

R.E.

'Candle' festivals

Light
Topic Web

Music

Singing nursery rhymes like
Twinkle, twinkle and
Hey, diddle diddle

Listening to Beethoven's
Moonlight Sonata
or *Morning* by Grieg

Plants need
light to grow

Simple circuits

Sharing poems
and stories

Effect of
light on
animals

Science

Language

Hibernation

Warning
lights/colours

Talking and writing
about celebrations
and festivals

Nocturnal

Prisms

Phrases including light

Technology

P.E. Dance/Drama

Making
something
with a
flashing light

Making a simple
time-measurer
e.g. candle-clock

Making 'distorted' mirror
reflections with body

Reflected shapes
with partner

Glossary

Advertisements   They are used to try to persuade you to buy something.

Auroras   Bands or streamers of light, that move across the sky in polar regions. Around the North Pole they are called the northern lights (aurora borealis), and around the South Pole they are called the southern lights (aurora australis).

Dawn   The beginning of a day.

Distort   To twist out of shape.

Dry dock   The part of a harbour where ships go for repair out of water.

Full moon   One of the four phases of the moon, that happens when the earth lies between the sun and the moon, so that the moon looks like a large, round disc.

Headlights   Strong lights on the front of cars and other vehicles.

Laser   A machine used for making light into a very narrow, powerful beam.

Lightbox   A box with a light inside for looking at slides.

Prism   A piece of glass with ends that are the same shape and size. Often, the ends are triangular in shape.

Reflect   To throw back light.

Slides   Photographs for showing on a screen.

Sparklers   Types of fireworks that throw out sparks.

Spectacular   Making a great show, or display.

Spectrum   The band of colours as seen in a rainbow.

Index